سو جاؤ، ننھے بھیڑئیے

Schlaf gut, kleiner Wolf

Ulrich Renz · Barbara Brinkmann

پرسکون نیند سو جاؤ، ننھے بھیڑئیے

Schlaf gut, kleiner Wolf

ترجمہ:

Muhammad Yahya, Dr. Laila Mushfa (اردو)

sefa

آڈیو بوک اور ویڈیو:

www.sefa-bilingual.com/bonus

مفت رسائی کے لیے پاس ورڈ:

اردو: **Sorry, audio or video is not yet available in this language.**

جرمن: **LWDE1314**

We are currently working on making as many of our bilingual books as possible available to you as audio books and videos. We kindly ask for your patience if there is no audio or video version in your language yet! You can keep up with the progress of our work on our website:
www.sefa-bilingual.com/languages

شب بخیر، ٹم! ہم کل اپنی تلاش جاری رکھیں گے۔
اب سکون سے سو جائو۔

Gute Nacht, Tim! Wir suchen morgen weiter.
Jetzt schlaf schön!

باہر پہلے ہی اندھیرا ہو گیا ہے۔

Draußen ist es schon dunkel.

ٹم کیا کر رہا ہے؟

Was macht Tim denn da?

وہ کھیل کے میدان میں جانے کے لیئے نکل رہا ہے۔
وہ یہاں کیا تلاش کر رہا ہے؟

Er geht raus, zum Spielplatz.

Was sucht er da?

ننھے بھیڑئیے!

وہ اس کے بغیر نہیں سو سکتا۔

Den kleinen Wolf!

Ohne den kann er nicht schlafen.

یہ کون آ رہا ہے؟

Wer kommt denn da?

میری! وہ اپنی گیند تلاش کر رہی ہے۔

Marie! Die sucht ihren Ball.

اور ٹوبی کیا ڈھونڈ رہا ہے؟

Und was sucht Tobi?

اپنا کھدائی کرنے والا آلہ۔

Seinen Bagger.

اور نالا کیا ڈھونڈ رہی ہے؟

Und was sucht Nala?

اپنی گڑیا۔

Ihre Puppe.

کیا بچوں کو بستر پہ نہیں جانا ہے؟
بلی بہت زیادہ حیران ہوئی۔

Müssen die Kinder nicht ins Bett?

Die Katze wundert sich sehr.

chez Martin
7
vitrerie

اب کون آ رہا ہے؟

Wer kommt denn jetzt?

ٹم کے امی اور ابو!
وہ اپنے ٹم کے بغیر نہیں سو سکتے۔

Die Mama und der Papa von Tim!
Ohne ihren Tim können sie nicht schlafen.

ان میں سے زیادہ تر لوگ آ رہے ہیں!
میری کے ابو، ٹوبی کے دادا اور نالا کی امی۔

Und da kommen noch mehr! Der Papa von Marie.
Der Opa von Tobi. Und die Mama von Nala.

اب جلدی بستر پہ جائو!

Jetzt aber schnell ins Bett!

شب بخیر، ٹم! کل ہمیں مزید تلاش نہیں کرنا ہوگا۔

Gute Nacht, Tim!

Morgen müssen wir nicht mehr suchen.

پرسکون نیند سو جاؤ، ننھے بھیڑئیے!

Schlaf gut, kleiner Wolf!

مصنفين

Ulrich Renz was born in Stuttgart, Germany, in 1960. After studying French literature in Paris he graduated from medical school in Lübeck and worked as head of a scientific publishing company. He is now a writer of non-fiction books as well as children's fiction books.

www.ulrichrenz.de

Barbara Brinkmann was born in Munich in 1969 and grew up in the foothills of the Bavarian Alps. She studied architecture in Munich and is currently a research associate in the Department of Architecture at the Technical University of Munich. She also works as a freelance graphic designer, illustrator, and author.

www.bcbrinkmann.de

Do you like drawing?

Here are the pictures from the story to color in:

www.sefa-bilingual.com/coloring

Enjoy!

جنگلی ہنس

مأخوذة عن قصة لهانز كريستيان اندرسن

► Recommended age: 4-5 and up

ہینس کرسٹن اینڈرسن کی کہانی جنگلی ہنس، دنیا کی مشہور ترین بامقصد پریوں کی کہانیوں میں سے ایک ہے۔ یہ کہانی انسانی ڈرامہ کے ہر موضوع ؛ خوف، بہادری، محبت، دھوکہ، جدائی، اور ملن کا بہت خوبصورتی سے احاطہ کرتی ہے۔

Available in your language?

► Check out with our „Language Wizard“:

www.sefa-bilingual.com/languages

My Most Beautiful Dream

► Reading age: 2-3 and up

Lulu can't fall asleep. All her cuddly toys are dreaming already – the shark, the elephant, the little mouse, the dragon, the kangaroo, and the lion cub. Even the bear has trouble keeping his eyes open...
Hey bear, will you take me along into your dream?
Thus begins a journey for Lulu that leads her through the dreams of her cuddly toys – and finally to her own most beautiful dream.

Available in your language?

► Check out with our „Language Wizard":

www.sefa-bilingual.com/languages

www.sefa-verlag.de

IT: Paul Bödeker, Freiburg, Germany

Font: Noto Sans

ISBN: 9783739919126

CPSIA information can be obtained
at www.ICGtesting.com
Printed in the USA
LVHW070729040423
743407LV00008B/197